Happy Handwriting

Practice Book 2

Series Editor: Dr Jane Medwell
Author: Annabel Gray

William Collins' dream of knowledge for all began with the publication of his first book in 1819. A self-educated mill worker, he not only enriched millions of lives, but also founded a flourishing publishing house. Today, staying true to this spirit, Collins books are packed with inspiration, innovation and practical expertise.

They place you at the centre of a world of possibility and give you exactly what you need to explore it.

Collins. Freedom to teach.

Published by Collins
An imprint of HarperCollins*Publishers*
The News Building, 1 London Bridge Street, London, SE1 9GF, UK

HarperCollins*Publishers*
Macken House, 39/40 Mayor Street Upper, Dublin 1, DO1 C9W8, Ireland

Browse the complete Collins catalogue at
collins.co.uk

10 9 8 7 6 5 4 3

ISBN 978-0-00-848581-8

British Library Cataloguing-in-Publication Data
A catalogue record for this publication is available from the British Library.

Series Editor: Dr Jane Medwell
Author: Annabel Gray
Specialist reviewer: Dr Mellissa Prunty
Publisher: Lizzie Catford
Product manager: Sarah Thomas
Project manager: Jayne Jarvis
Development editor: Jane Cotter
Copyeditor: Oriel Square Ltd.
Proofreader: Oriel Square Ltd.
Cover and internal design and icons: Sarah-Leigh Wills at Happydesigner
Cover artwork: Jouve India Pvt. Ltd.
Illustrations: Jouve India Pvt. Ltd.
Typesetter: Jouve India Pvt. Ltd.
Production controller: Alhady Ali
Printed and bound in the UK using 100% renewable electricity at Martins the Printers Ltd.

Trace over and practise the joins.

ai ay   ai ay   ai ay

Use the pictures to help you complete the words. Remember to join the missing letters.

tr __ __ n   pl __ __

Trace over and copy the sentence.

I play with my train in the rain.

a b c d e f g h i j k l m n o p q r s t u v w x y z

Trace over and practise the joins.

ie ue ae   *ie ue ae*

ie ue ae

Use the pictures to help you complete the words. Remember to join the missing letters.

p_ _

bl_ _

Trace over and copy the sentence.

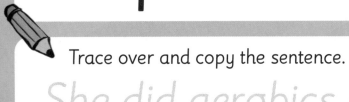

She did aerobics and ate a blue pie.

a b c d e f g h i j k l m n o p q r s t u v w x y z

Trace over and practise the joins.

ir ar ur   *ir ar ur*

ir ar ur

Use the pictures to help you complete the words. Remember to join the missing letters.

g _ _ l

c _ _

Trace over and copy the sentence.

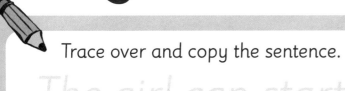

The girl can start your car.

a b c d e f g h i j k l m n o p q r s t u v w x y z

Trace over and practise the joins.

ch th ch th ch th

Use the pictures to help you complete the words. Remember to join the missing letters.

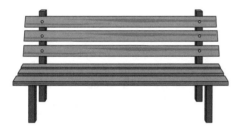

ben__

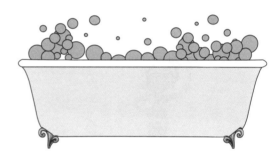

ba__

Trace over and copy the sentence.

Having a bath with cheese is strange!

a b c d e f g h i j k l m n o p q r s t u v w x y z

Trace over and practise the joins.

al all alk   *al all alk*

al all alk

Use the pictures to help you complete the words. Remember to join the missing letters.

b _ _ _

w _ _ _

Trace over and copy the sentence.

I am too tall to walk on the wall.

a b c d e f g h i j k l m n o p q r s t u v w x y z

Trace over and practise the joins.

oa ow out oa ow out

oa ow out

Use the pictures to help you complete the words. Remember to join the missing letters.

g _ _ t

cl _ _ n

Trace over and copy the sentence.

The clown shouted at the goat.

a b c d e f g h i j k l m n o p q r s t u v w x y z

Trace over and practise the joins.

we oe ve   we oe ve

we oe ve

Use the pictures to help you complete the words. Remember to join the missing letters.

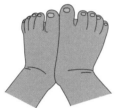

t _ _ s   do _ _

Trace over and copy the sentence.

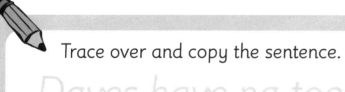

Doves have no toes so wear no shoes.

a b c d e f g h i j k l m n o p q r s t u v w x y z

Trace over and practise the joins.

wh oh wh oh wh oh

Use the pictures to help you complete the words. Remember to join the missing letters.

__ale

J__n

Trace over and copy the sentence.

This whale is named John.

a b c d e f g h i j k l m n o p q r s t u v w x y z

Trace over and practise the numbers.

1 2 3 4 5

6 7 8 9 10

Trace over and complete the missing numbers.

0 1 _ 3 4 _ 6 7 _ 9

0 _ 2 _ 4 5 _ 7 8 _

Trace over and copy the sequences.

0 2 4 6 8
1 3 5 7 9

a b c d e f g h i j k l m n o p q r s t u v w x y z

Trace over the capital letters.

A B C D E F G H I J

K L M N O P Q R

S T U V W X Y Z

Trace over and copy.

Mr Miss Mrs Ms

Copy out the names, adding the capital letters.

mrs singh   miss james   mr griffiths

a b c d e f g h i j k l m n o p q r s t u v w x y z

Trace over and practise the joins.

ice ace ce   ice ace ce

ice ace ce

Use the pictures to help you complete the words. Remember to join the missing letters.

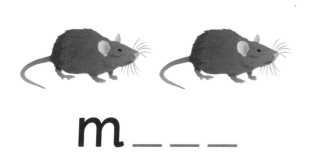

m _ _ _

f _ _ _

Trace over and copy the sentence.

The mice had nice faces.

a b c d e f g h i j k l m n o p q r s t u v w x y z

Trace over and practise the joins.

ea ad ea ad ea ad

Use the pictures to help you complete the words. Remember to join the missing letters.

d r __ __ m

s __ __

Trace over and copy the sentence.

I had a sad dream.

a b c d e f g h i j k l m n o p q r s t u v w x y z

Trace over and practise the joins.

dg ng dg ng dg ng

Use the pictures to help you complete the words. Remember to join the missing letters.

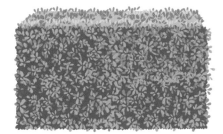

he__e

wi__

Trace over and copy the sentence.

A bird flapped its wings on the hedge.

a b c d e f g h i j k l m n o p q r s t u v w x y z

Trace over and practise the joins.

igh ing   igh ing

igh ing

Use the pictures to help you complete the words. Remember to join the missing letters.

n___t

s____

Trace over and copy the sentence.

I sing during the night in moonlight.

a b c d e f g h i j k l m n o p q r s t u v w x y z

Trace over and practise the joins.

ee ea ey   *ee ea ey*

ee ea ey

Use the pictures to help you complete the words. Remember to join the missing letters.

b _ _

p _ _ ch

Trace over and copy the sentence.

The bee eyed a peach.

a b c d e f g h i j k l m n o p q r s t u v w x y z

Trace over and practise the joins.

oo oa oo oa oo oa

Use the pictures to help you complete the words. Remember to join the missing letters.

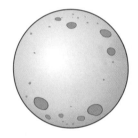

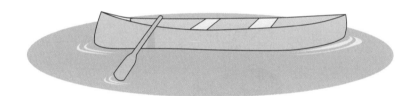

m __ __ n   b __ __ t

Trace over and copy the sentence.

I had a boat on the moon.

a b c d e f g h i j k l m n o p q r s t u v w x y z

Trace over and practise the joins.

wa wo vi   wa wo vi

wa wo vi

Use the pictures to help you complete the words. Remember to join the missing letters.

__ter

__rm

Trace over and copy the sentence.

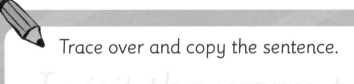

I visit the worm to give it water.

a b c d e f g h i j k l m n o p q r s t u v w x y z

Trace over and practise the joins.

au aw or   *au aw or*

au aw or

Use the pictures to help you complete the words. Remember to join the missing letters.

s _ _

do _ _

Trace over and copy the sentence.

My aunt put the saw by the door.

a b c d e f g h i j k l m n o p q r s t u v w x y z

Trace over and practise the joins.

an mb wr wh   an mb wr wh

an mb wr wh

Use the pictures to help you complete the words. Remember to join the missing letters.

la___

__ite

Trace over and copy the sentence.

The lamb stands when I write.

a b c d e f g h i j k l m n o p q r s t u v w x y z

21

Trace over and practise the joins.

air ear our air ear our

air ear our

Use the pictures to help you complete the words. Remember to join the missing letters.

p _ _ _

ch _ _ _ _

Trace over and copy the sentence.

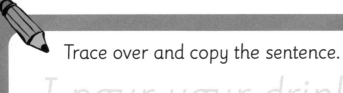

I pour your drink at the chair.

a b c d e f g h i j k l m n o p q r s t u v w x y z

Trace over and practise the joins.

ily ely kly   *ily ely kly*

ily ely kly

23

Use the pictures to help you complete the words. Remember to join the missing letters.

l_ _ _

pric_ _ _

Trace over and copy the sentence.

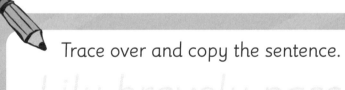

Lily bravely passed a prickly bush.

a b c d e f g h i j k l m n o p q r s t u v w x y z

23

Trace over and practise the joins.

of ful to at   of ful to at

of ful to at

Use the pictures to help you complete the words. Remember to join the missing letters.

_ _ _ l

c _ _

Trace over and copy the sentence.

The cat was too full of food to move.

a b c d e f g h i j k l m n o p q r s t u v w x y z

Trace over and practise the joins.

ui aw ip   *ui aw ip*

ui aw ip

Use the pictures to help you complete the words. Remember to join the missing letters.

fr__t

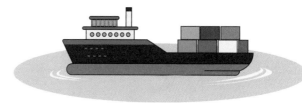

sh__

Trace over and copy the sentence.

Use a straw to drink fruit juice on a ship.

a b c d e f g h i j k l m n o p q r s t u v w x y z

Trace over and practise the joins.

ck el il   *ck el il*

ck el il

Use the pictures to help you complete the words. Remember to join the missing letters.

du_ _

h_ _l

Trace over and copy the sentence.

The duck fell down the hill.

a b c d e f g h i j k l m n o p q r s t u v w x y z

Trace over and practise the joins.

on op wi   on op wi

on op wi

Use the pictures to help you complete the words. Remember to join the missing letters.

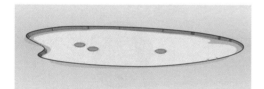

p_ _d   sh_ _

Trace over and copy the sentence.

I drove to the shop one windy day.

a b c d e f g h i j k l m n o p q r s t u v w x y z

27

Trace over and practise the joins.

ol ob ot   *ol ob ot*

ol ob ot

Use the pictures to help you complete the words. Remember to join the missing letters.

s _ _

h _ _ _

Trace over and copy the sentence.

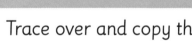

My doll sobs if it is hot.

a b c d e f g h i j k l m n o p q r s t u v w x y z

Trace over and practise the joins.

ag dd ug   ag dd ug

ag dd ug

Use the pictures to help you complete the words. Remember to join the missing letters.

b _ _

te _ _ y

Trace over and copy the sentence.

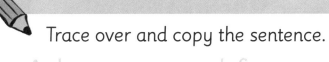

A bug jumped from my teddy to my bag.

a b c d e f g h i j k l m n o p q r s t u v w x y z

Trace over and practise the joins.

oc og va   *oc og va*

oc og va

Use the pictures to help you complete the words. Remember to join the missing letters.

s _ _ k

fr _ _

Trace over and copy the sentence.

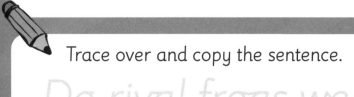

Do rival frogs wear socks on logs?

a b c d e f g h i j k l m n o p q r s t u v w x y z

Trace over and practise the letters.

b g j p q x y z s

Use the pictures to help you complete the words.

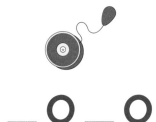

_ o _ o

_ o o k

Practise the unjoined letters.

b g j p q x y z s

Trace over and copy the sentence.

The green bear eats a pear with jam.

a b c d e f g h i j k l m n o p q r s t u v w x y z

Trace over and copy.

hall _____   they _____
by _____   because _____
why _____   through _____

My tall letters are . . . 😦 😐 🙂

My tails are . . . 😦 😐 🙂

Trace over and copy the sentence.

The red fox ran away quickly.

I joined some letters. 😦 😐 🙂

My spaces are right. 😦 😐 🙂

What can I do better?

My handwriting target is:

a b c d e f g h i j k l m n o p q r s t u v w x y z